Rising Stars 2016

Organised by New Ashgate Gallery
in partnership with the University for the Creative Arts

The competition is supported by the Billmeir Charitable Trust

New Ashgate Gallery
Waggon Yard
Farnham
Surrey GU9 7PS

newashgate.org.uk
Registered charity no. 274326

Editor and design: Lucy Payne
Cover image: Melissa Yarlett, *Forrest Cluster Earrings*, silver

New Ashgate Gallery

UCA
university for the **creative arts**

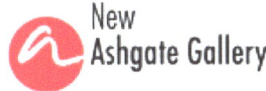

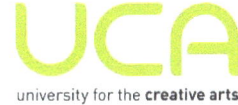

Celebrating the emerging talent

Rising Stars is a platform to view and collect some of the most exciting new work by emerging talent across the UK. This curated, selling exhibition enables new artists and makers to access the market place and collectors during these challenging economic times. The artwork in the exhibition is available for sale and every sale supports the artist.

The artists and makers were selected following an open call for applications. The selection panel consisted of Rebecca Skeels, Post Graduate Subject & Senior Tutor for University of Creative Arts Farnham; Caitlin Heffernan, Visual Officer for Surrey Arts and Caroline Jackman, artist and arts manager.

Opportunities such as *Rising Stars* are needed more than ever, as arts funding is being questioned and art organisations sometimes focus on established names that are less risky than presenting recent graduates or students. The winner of the *Rising Stars* Professional Development Award will be announced in the Rising Stars private view on 4 March and she/he will receive a cash prize and a solo exhibition in the gallery. We hope that this will have a significant impact on the winner's career. The exhibition also has a related professional development programme that supports all emerging artists and makers – the participants of this exhibition and all regional new talent.

Rising Stars is produced by New Ashgate Gallery in partnership with the University for the Creative Arts. It is supported by the Billmeir Charitable Trust. We would like to thank UCA and the Billmeir Charitable Trust for their continuing support for the programme.

I hope that you enjoy the exhibition.

Dr Outi Remes
Gallery Director
New Ashgate Gallery Trust

Shortlisted artists and makers

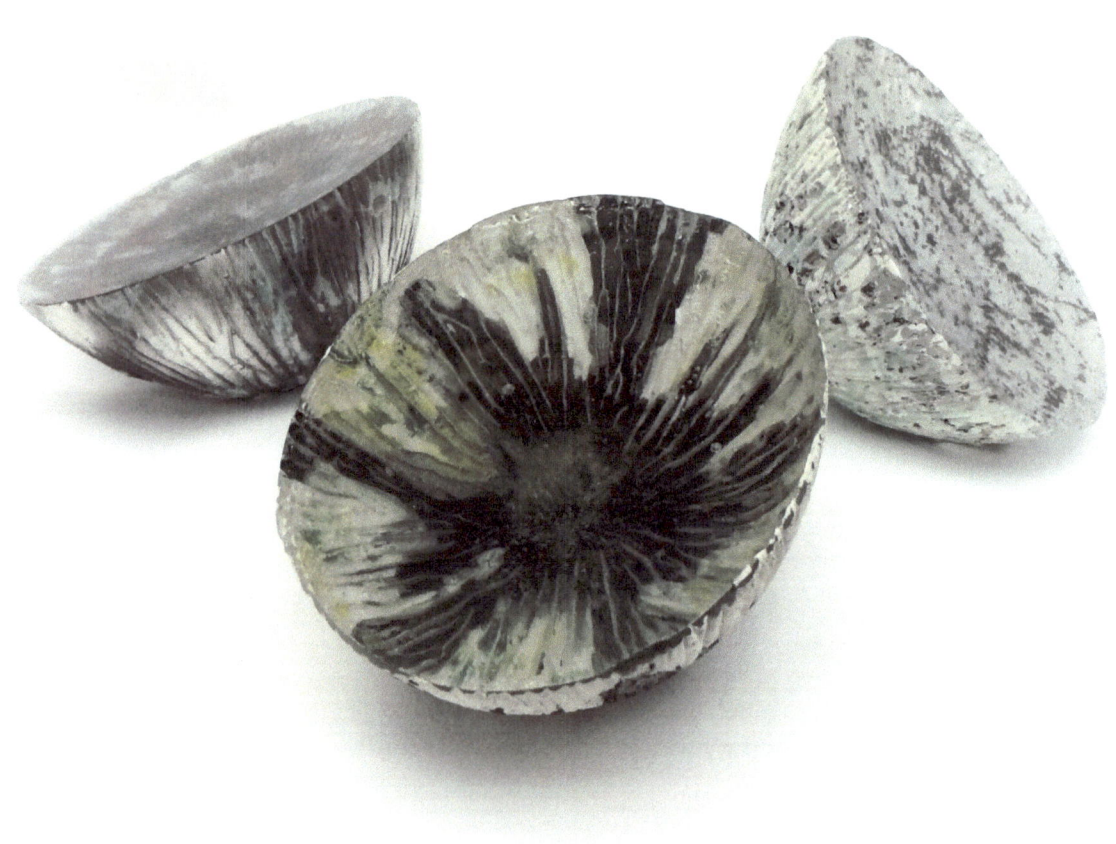

Mike Barrett

2015 MA Glass, UCA Farnham

2015 Btech 3 Kiln Formed Glass, WAES

Mike is exploring the illusory transparency of glass, a material that deceives us with false appearances. It looks like we could pass through it, yet we cannot do so. It is arguably a composite of rocks and metals, yet it is transparent, not opaque. Only when we touch it, bump into it or pick it up, do we encounter forgiving fragility, hardness, coldness and weight and begin to believe the truth of its material component history.

We live in an increasingly crowded, cluttered and noisy world with few opportunities to be truly alone with ourselves. The transparency of glass is capable of creating a moment of perplexity where we doubt the evidence of our eyes, in which attention is captured and a sense of wonder created. Within Mike's work he explores that pause and moment of openness to create work that draws people into a contemplative space. He is currently creating glass pieces that give the impression of being made from other material – thin fragile shells apparently filled with water. They give us that entranced rock pool experience of childhood, the one where we stare into a small world to watch the life within and, just for a moment, the world stops. Most of the pieces can be held in cupped hands and brought close, enabling an easy slide into personal and private reflection. There are associations with the use of Chawans in the Japanese tea ceremony and also devotional icons used in private prayer.

Image: *Three Shell Forms*, kiln formed glass and enamel. Photographer: Mike Barrett

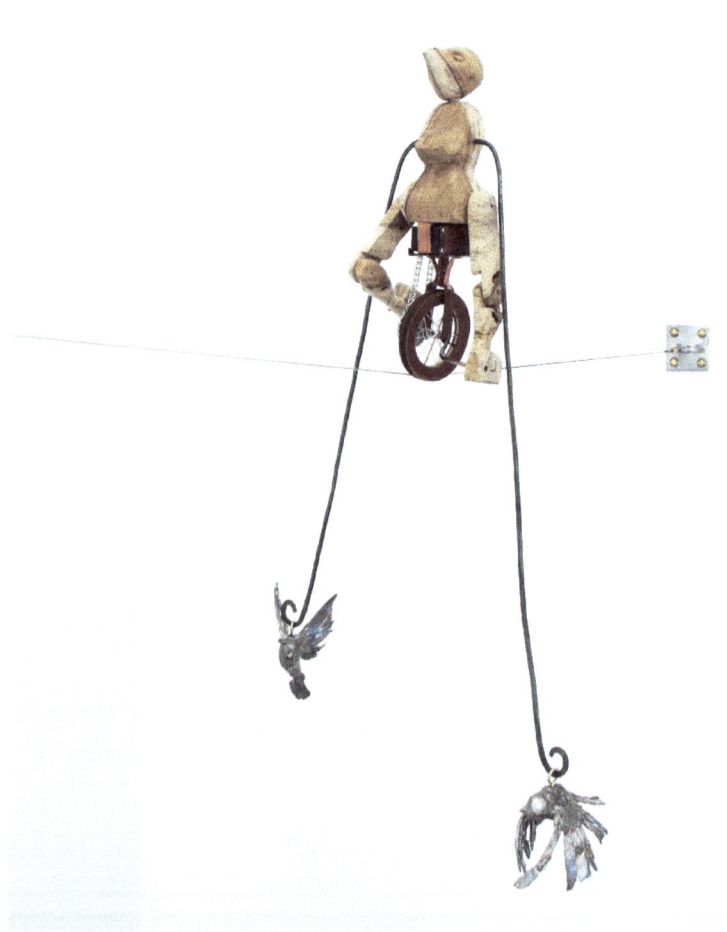

Charlotte Biszewski

2015 MA Multi-disciplinary Print Making, University of the West of England, Bristol

2012 BA Spanish and Portuguese, The University of Manchester

Charlotte is a Bristol based installation artist, puppeteer, book artist and print-maker, whose work investigates narrative, characters and imaginary worlds. Hand-carved puppets and wooden kinetic toys make up the body of her work, with these she explores fantasy narratives and develops imaginary worlds. They play with movement and interactive digital-technologies, creating enjoyable installations. In these she aims to engage with her audience, recapture the magic of childhood and not be too serious.

Wood is an integral element; it feeds and directs every discipline of her practice. Charlotte enjoys the challenge of its limitations and it's tactile, simple beauty. She seeks to display and acknowledge the handmade imperfections of her work, reminding audiences of the materials used and the craft in its creation.

Bird on a Wire combines this love of the hand-made rickety toys, those found in peculiar museum collections, with our never-ending fascination of technology and mechanics. It explores the circus, why we remain amazed by the tightrope and enthralled by the marvels of a good, old-fashioned balancing act.

Image: *Bird on a wire*, wood, copper & lead. Photographer: Charlotte Biszewski

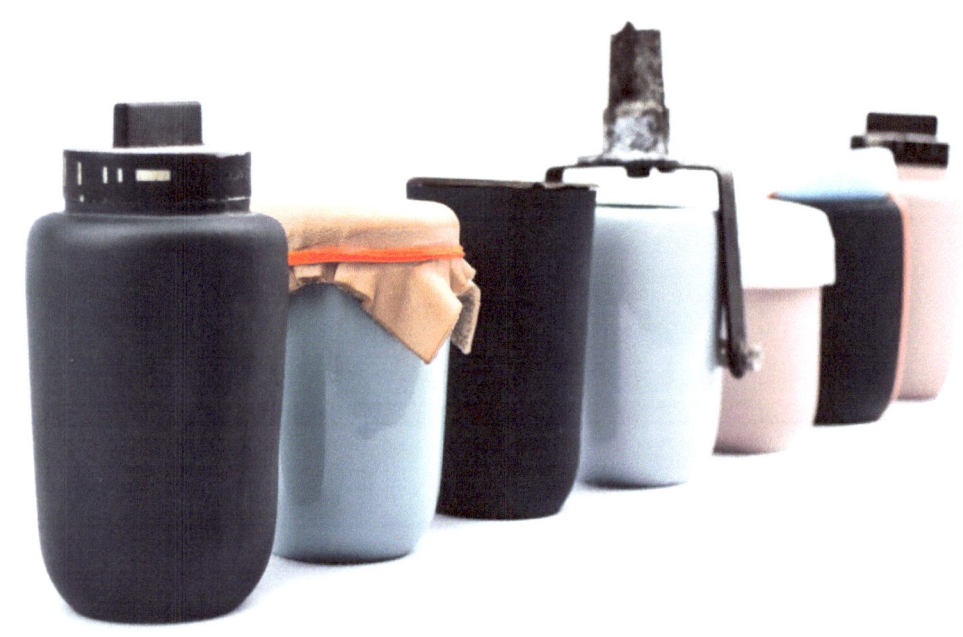

Aimee Bollu

2014 BA (Hons) Decorative Arts, Nottingham Trent University

Aimee Bollu is a collector, a gatherer, an arranger of the things people have discarded and forgotten. She seeks out objects that have fallen out of use, out of society, and brings them back to life. Through the creation of hybrid objects, incorporating these found elements and newly made vessel forms, the disregarded items become meaningful once more, and possess a new value.

Bollu has an instinctive approach to design; she scours the streets, engrossed in the process of walking, searching, and responding to the detritus of urban life. The found objects, once full of purpose but now detached from their original meaning, take place within her collection and wait. Then comes the act of making; repetitive process of drawing, mould-making, slip casting, turning and finishing. Simple vessel forms, in a variety of hues and materials form the support, the framework for the display of the found objects. The found and the made are combined to become a 'new thing' with echoes of a past life, and the possibilities of a new one.

These new pieces are intriguing and curious. Unexpected materials, and the ordinary, adorn the almost-bare forms. Rusted and twisted metal emerges from candy-pop porcelain suggesting a handle. Neon twine encircles draped leather, forming drum-like surface over a curved vessel. An oven knob nestles into the aperture of a turned wooden pot. There is nothing extraneous in the combinations; these items have been seemingly destined to be collaged into their new form.

Image: *Curious Boxes*, slipcast porcelain. Photographer: Yasmin Ensor

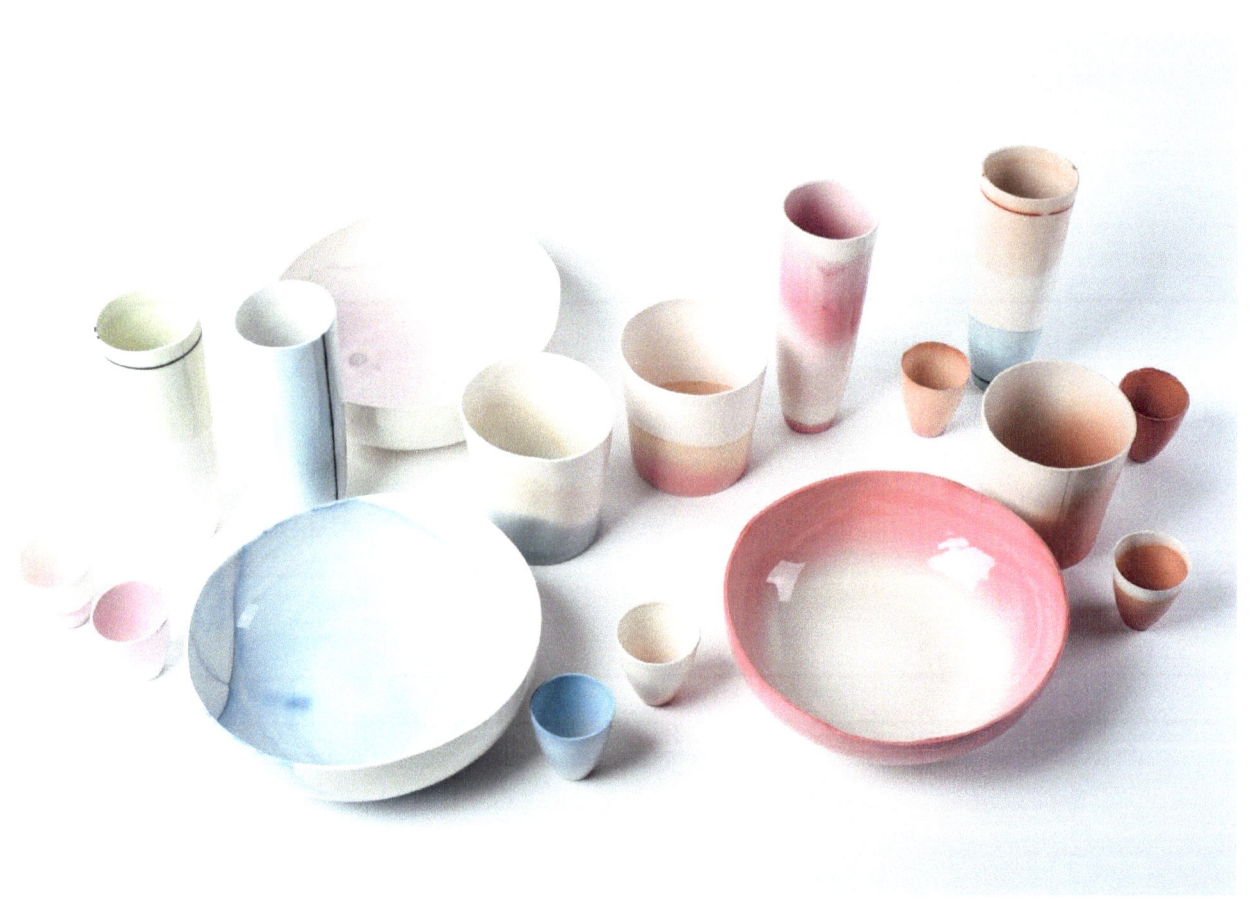

Emma Buckley

2015 BA (Hons) Three Dimensional Design: Idea Material Object, Bath School of Art & Design, Bath Spa University

Dye Lines is a range of intriguing and colourful earthenware reveals the discovery of a new process using dyes traditionally used in the textile industry. A highly soluble dye, conventionally used for tie-dye or batik, is absorbed through a sandblasted gap in the glaze, dyeing the ceramics vibrant colours that are unobtainable using traditional methods.

The shape and size of the gap serves as the 'blueprint' for the final result, allowing a measure of control in a largely unpredictable process. Over time however - the patterns change - the saturated colour gradually becomes muted as the water carrying particles of dye slowly evaporate through the point from which it entered, leaving the residue of dye where it once existed.

Image: *Dye Lines, ceramics & textile dye.* Photographer: Emma Buckley

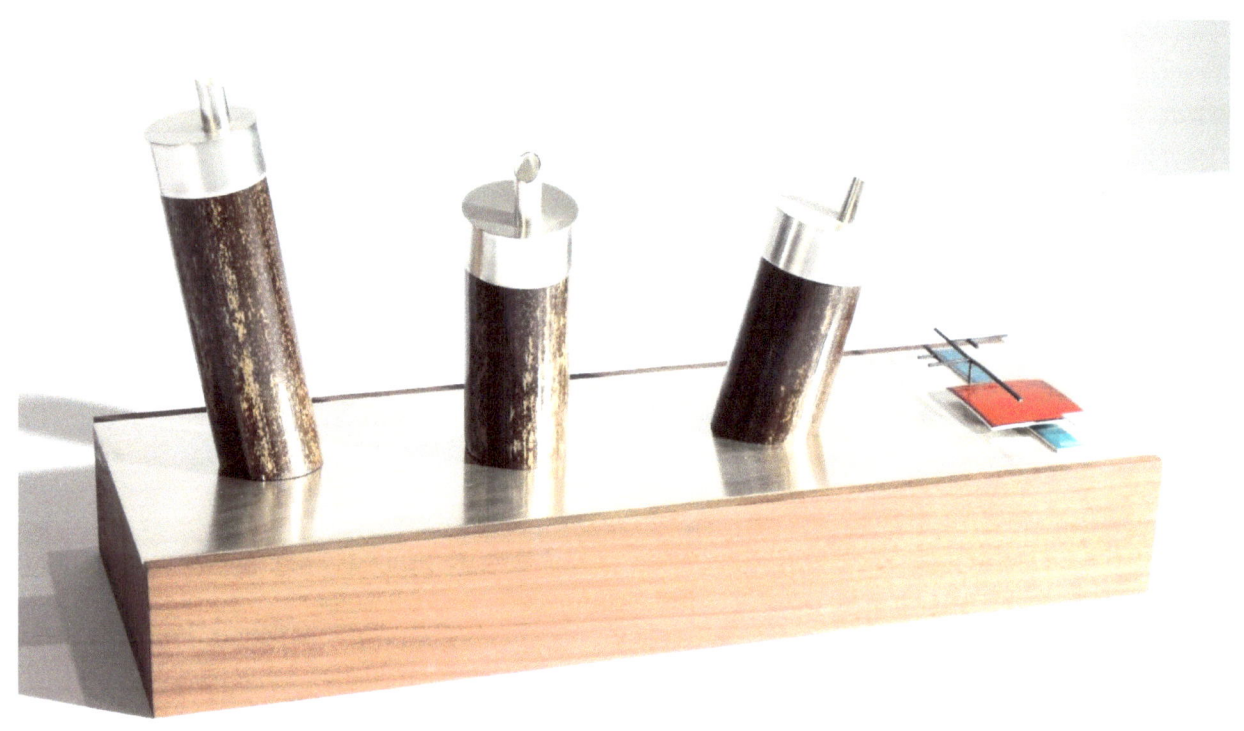

Rachel Butlin

2015 BA (Hons) Decorative Arts, Nottingham Trent University

Rachel Butlin has a passion for materials allowing playful processes to be explored throughout pieces. She produces a range of high end, mixed material, functional and wearable objects for the high-end jewellery and restaurant markets.

Rachel seeks to challenge the concepts of contemporary, interactive and wearable objects. The pieces are all handmade, carefully considering material combination, including bamboo and silver.

Rachel's unique brand identity 'MAKE IT.EAT IT.WEAR IT', perfectly describes the playful nature of each and every piece.

Image: *Wearables Collection and Interactive Station Collection*, silver, bamboo, glass, enamel. Photographer: Rachel Butlin

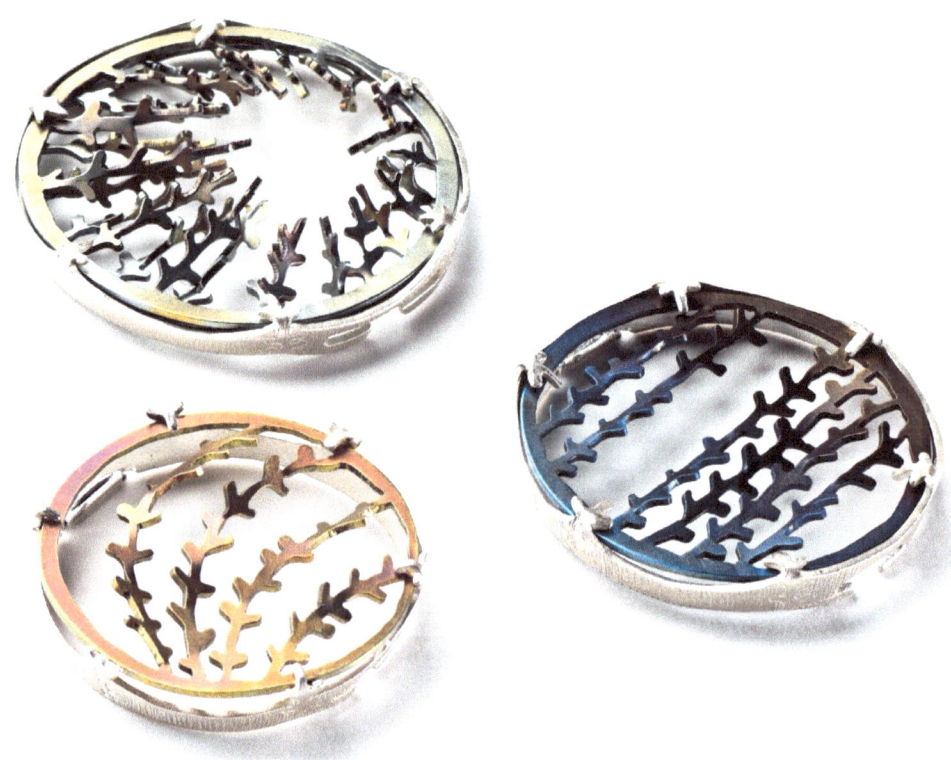

Karen Elizabeth Donovan

2014 MA Fine Arts in Jewellery Design, Edinburgh College of Art, Edinburgh University

2012 BA (Hons) Science in Studio Art, Jewellery and Metalsmithing, Skidmore College, New York

Karen choses to employ plant forms in her work because plants define the character of place. Scotland has an incredible history of stories and lives. There is a tangible history of folklore, jewellery and plants. Karen enjoys exploring this history while learning more about it. She has come to appreciate the importance of the Scottish heather as a significant fixture in the landscape of Scotland. Heather is also, like titanium, lightweight, strong, durable and springy. Titanium presents wonderful challenges to overcome and work around, and gives the strength to delicate wirework and piercing. Colour and pattern are integral to her work and are developed through the close study of plants and created by the attributes of titanium. As Karen's work continues to develop, she has incorporated more gold, which historically held it's own role in the ever-changing Scottish landscape. Karen finds the disparity between gold and titanium to be fascinating and continues to work on this relationship.

Karen's work is made by hand; she bends all the wires into shapes with just a pair of pliers. She then connects it all together and anodises it to give it the beautiful colours. Karen currently works out of Process Studios in Edinburgh, where she is constantly inspired by the artists around her and the variety of flora in Holyrood Park.

Image: *Wild Heather Brooches*, anodized titanium and silver. Photographer: Shannon Tofts

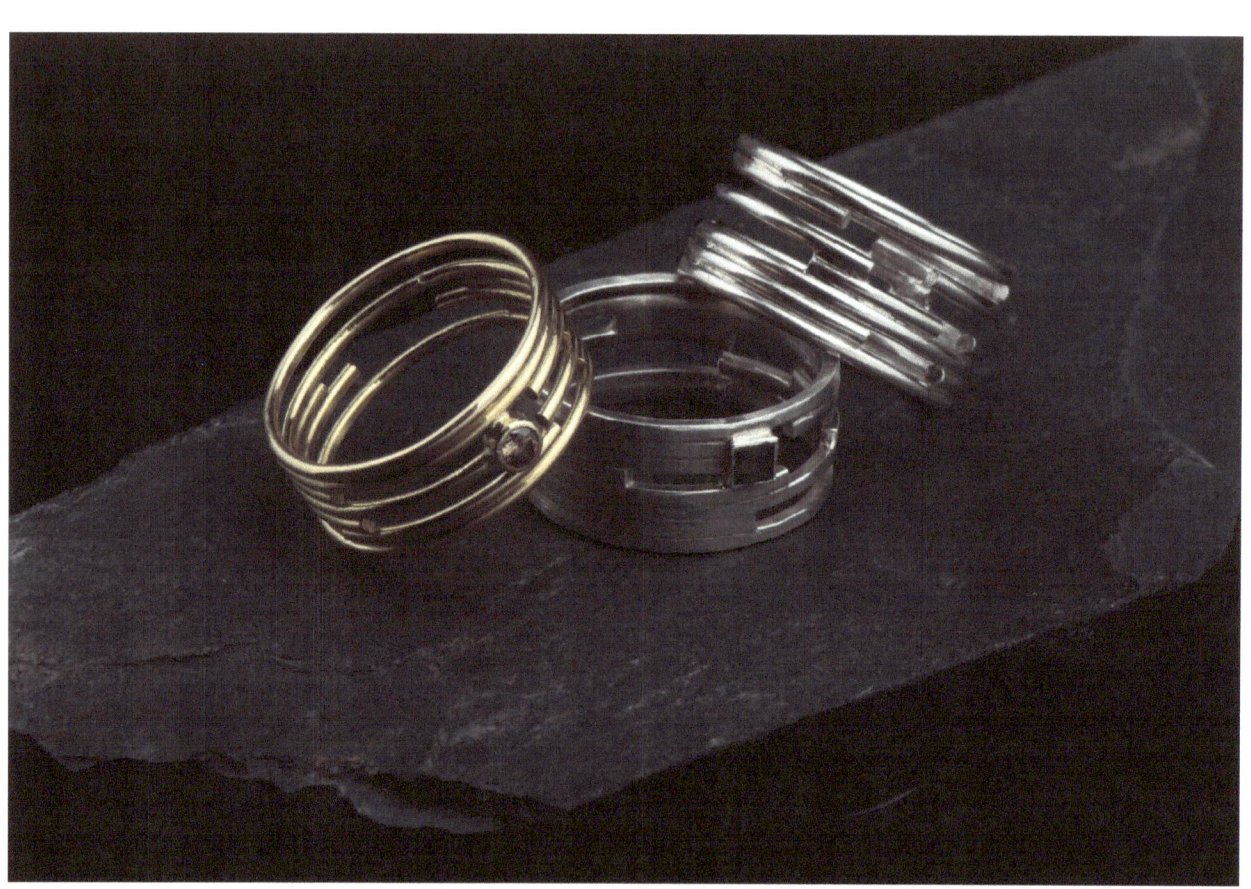

Carol Hunt

2015 MA By Project, the Cass School of Art and Design, London Met University

2001 BA (Hons) Management Studies, Nottingham University

Carol is fascinated by the meanings that jewellery objects can take on for us, being intensely personal expressions of self, and in their ability to become symbols of people, places and memories. Her work seeks to explore narrative and memory to comment on the human experience in an abstract manner using material, form and particularly line.

Contrasts are ever present in her work, of light and dark, strength and delicacy, what is displayed and what is hidden, the precious and non-precious. Carol chooses her materials for the meanings, memories and significance they hold, some experimental work exploring combinations and contrasts of precious and non-precious materials including leather with gold and concrete and diamonds.

Carol's work is handmade and uses traditional jewellery techniques such as fabrication, forging and stone setting as well as more experimental techniques relevant to working with specific materials and combining them with precious metals.

Recent work explores her intensely personal memories of a life event expressed through line tension and delicacy, and resulting in the Shards collection. The Vessels series employs her characteristic contemporary aesthetic with reference to secret messages and meanings, allowing the wearer to decide their own story.

Ultimately Carol aims to create contemporary jewellery objects that are treasured by their wearers.

Image: *Shards Ring Collection II,* sterling silver and tourmaline, 18ct gold and brown diamond. Photographer: James Champion

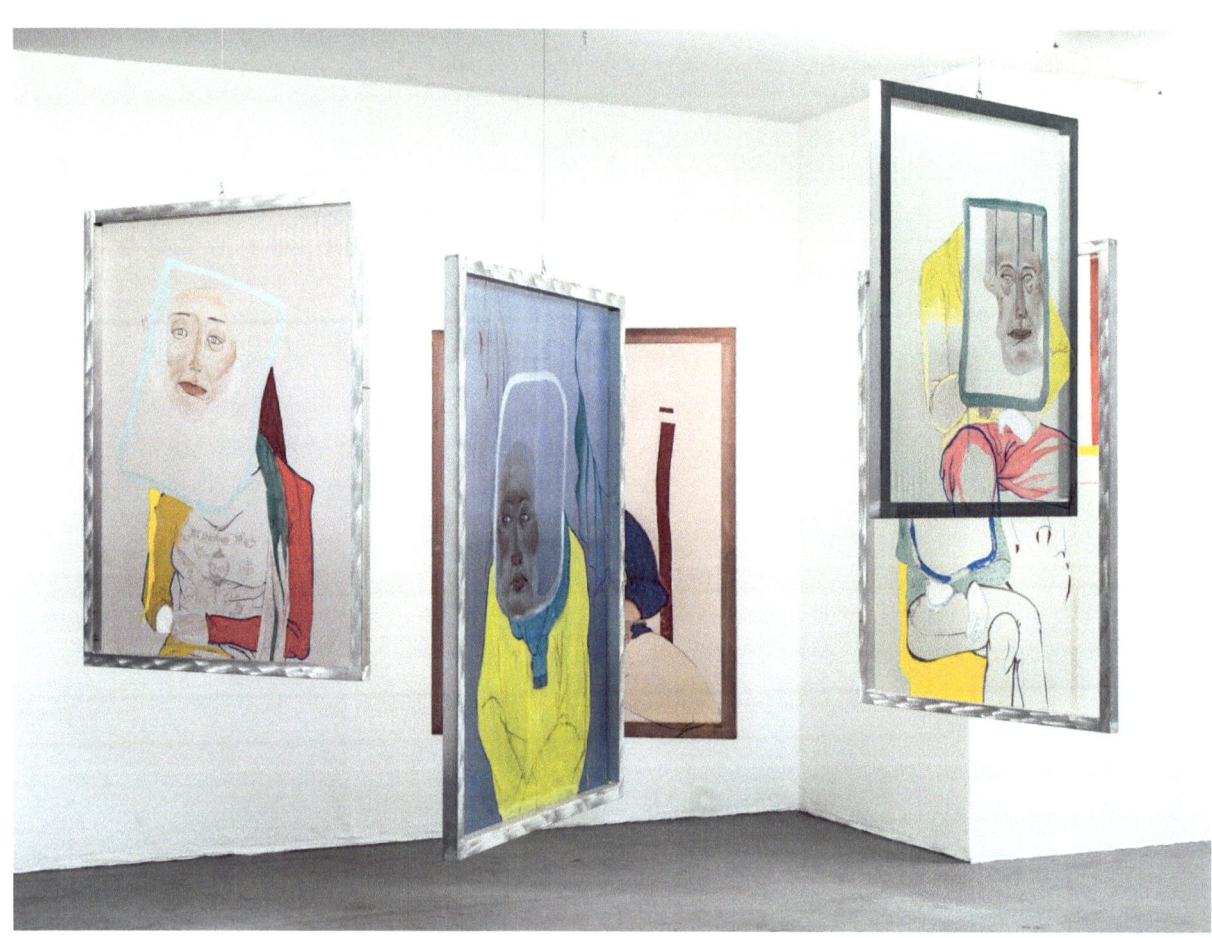

Tae Yeon Kim

2016 MFA Painting, Slade School of Fine Art
2013 MA Fine Art in Oriental Painting, Seoul National University
2009 BA Fine Art in Oriental Painting, Seoul National University

Tae's work deals with human interactions and ephermal encounters using the same disjunction between the ideal world of traditional Korean painting and the reality of everyday relationship. Uncovering, exploring and broadening the ambiguous boundary of relationships through ever-changing surfaces and multisensory stimuli are at the core of Tae's current practice. The interest has recently taken Tae to explore the most elusive encounter of meeting someone new; first impressions and the inevitable changes as the relationships deepen.

To capture the sensual and spiritual effects when encountering a person, the artist has made a series of paintings that are portraits but have been driven by memory rather than direct observation. The paintings were produced purely from trying to recall impressions. These paintings are installed as a screen, dividing the space and urging the viewers to walk through and experience the paintings in an ever-changing way. The versatile materiality of the fabric and its transparency is creating a physically dividing, yet visually accessible maze-like space where the ephemeral memory rests.

Image: *Resting The Passing,* pigment on fabric. Photographer: Peter Hope

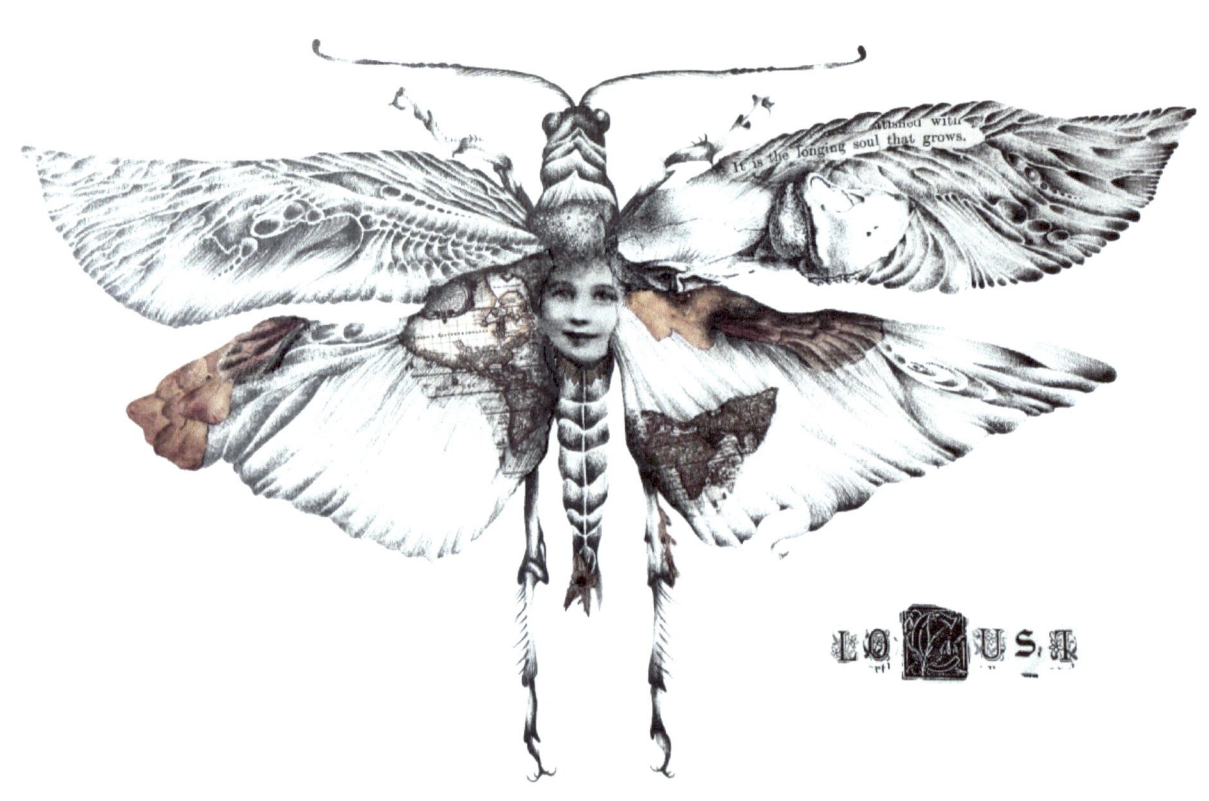

Georgia Lingwood

2014 BA (Hons) Fine Art, Kingston University

The Victorian era is of great inspiration to Georgia's work, especially the fairy tales by the Grimm brothers, strange objects found within cabinets of curiosity and the eerie forms of expressing the afterlife through the use of early photographic techniques.

Georgia is a collector of all sorts of oddities such as 'memento mori' photographs, aged love letters, pocket books of poetry, animal skulls, taxidermy birds and rabbit claws, to mention a few. Each of these individual objects tells a story and these ideas are incorporated into her drawings, sculptures and photographs. Alongside these papers she incorporates dried then pressed leaves and flowers, their tiny veins acting like the wings of insects. Within all of her illustrations she places a sentence. Inspired by a four year old boy who has autism she has created her latest series of drawings entitled my *Bestiary,* based on the characters that the child describes. His words give Georgia the keys to worlds of imaginary stories and images she could not create alone. She works with the child one on one at his school and throughout the day she keeps a notebook on her to jot down anything he says that fascinates her or inspires a character. The first piece she ever created depicted one of his extraordinary imaginings. It said: "The baby sleeps inside the elephant's trunk, swimming in the ocean with the jellyfish."

Each drawing is completed using a HB graphite pencil partnered with a selection of collaged papers and vintage pieces collected over the years.

Image: *Locust,* pencil drawing with antique collage and real flowers. Photographer: Georgia Lingwood

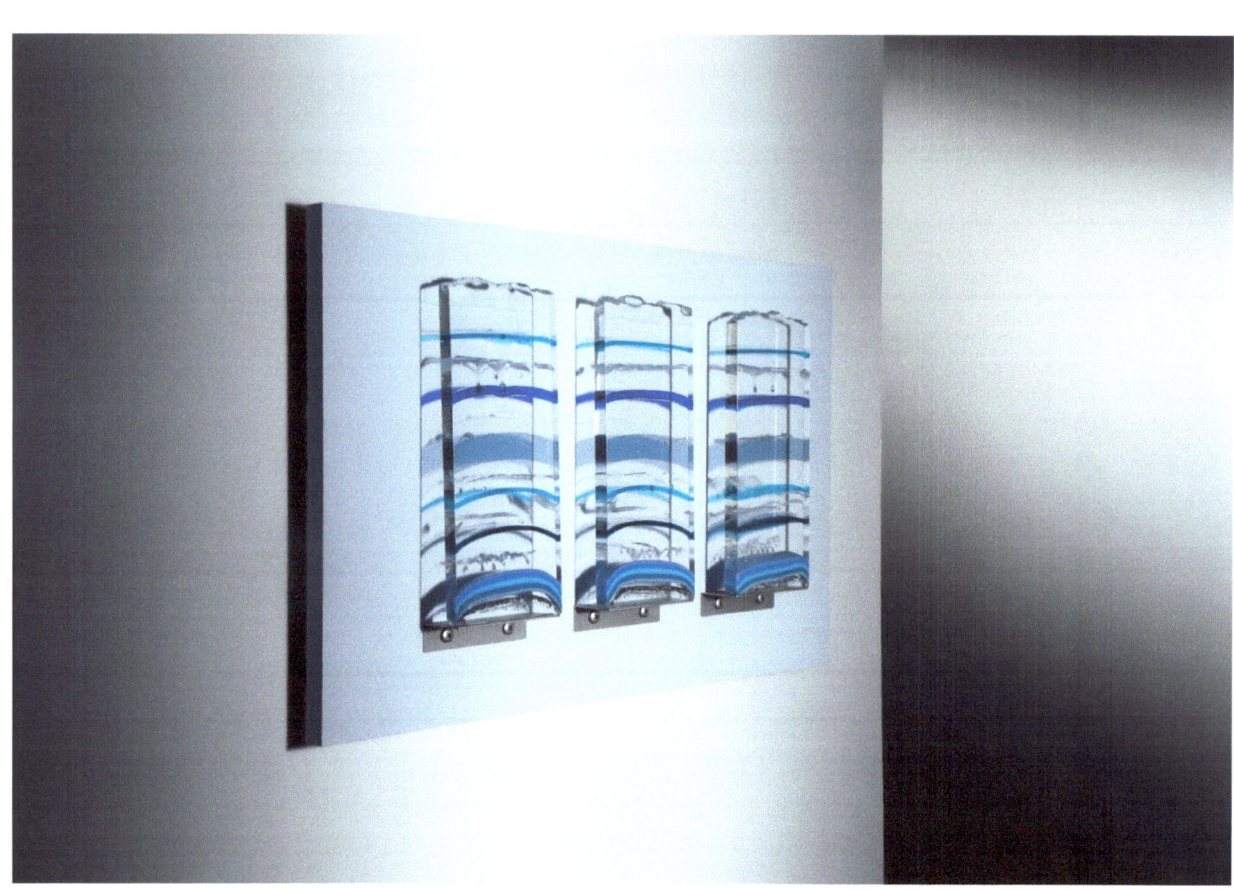

Joanna Lloyd

2015 MA in Contemporary Craft (Glass), UCA Farnham

2013 BA (Hons) Three Dimensional Design – Glass, UCA Farnham

We all leave a trace, a fragment, a memory. This concept can be described by the Latin word 'vestigium' which means 'a trace or a footprint', and to Joanna that encompasses the themes she has been researching for this body of work.

Originally an archaeologist, she has a strong interest in the past and the evidence beneath our feet, which may or may not be visible or legible. All humanity leaves a trace both as individuals and communities, the detritus maybe deeply buried. We cannot always identify artefacts and they can offer a tantalising glimmer of a life lived.

Glass is a particularly evocative and appropriate material to use in creating pieces inspired by fragments, traces, and memories.

Joanna has developed connections with archaeologists to advance her research. They have allowed her to cast textures during excavations, such as the Tudor Queens Apartments & medieval remains at Woking Palace, which she has used in her glass.

The glass processes used include lamp working, sandblasting, engraving, casting with multiple kiln firings, cold working and polishing.

Image: *Vestigium* series, glass. Photographer: Simon Bruntnell

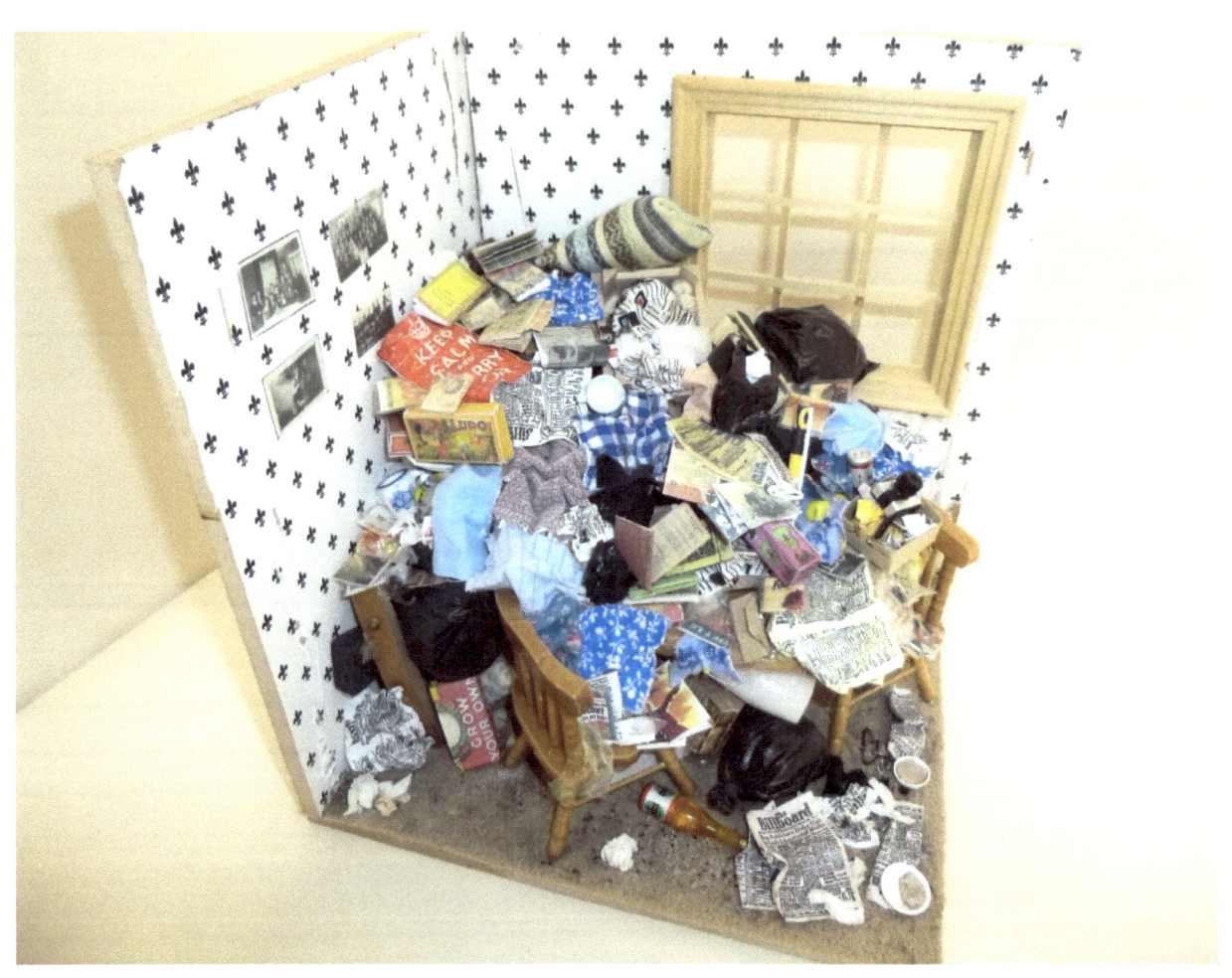

Sarah Luxford

2015 BA (Hons) Fine Art, Northbrook University Campus, Worthing

Within Sarah's practice she uses miniature scale to prompt childhood memories of naivety and innocent aspects of herself and others that she feels becomes lost as adults. Simple as these works might first appear, they explore a symptom of modern society.

Your thoughts and daydreams are chaotically lost as you get captured within the visual arrangement that is in a careful sense of organisation. They may leave you exhausted and suffocated, draining the thought process to absorb the visual impact and captivated thoughts imprisoned are being trapped into a downward spiral. The everlasting hole displays no escape or security and no elastic sponge of a safety net to soften the blow.

The emotions are locked and generations of memories that are firmly grounded connect to family history, making the absence of family members incredibly hard to comprehend.

Sarah's work aims to capture experiences within a single moment whilst those embedded memories last forever.

Image: *Dining Table,* mixed medium. Photographer: Sarah Luxford

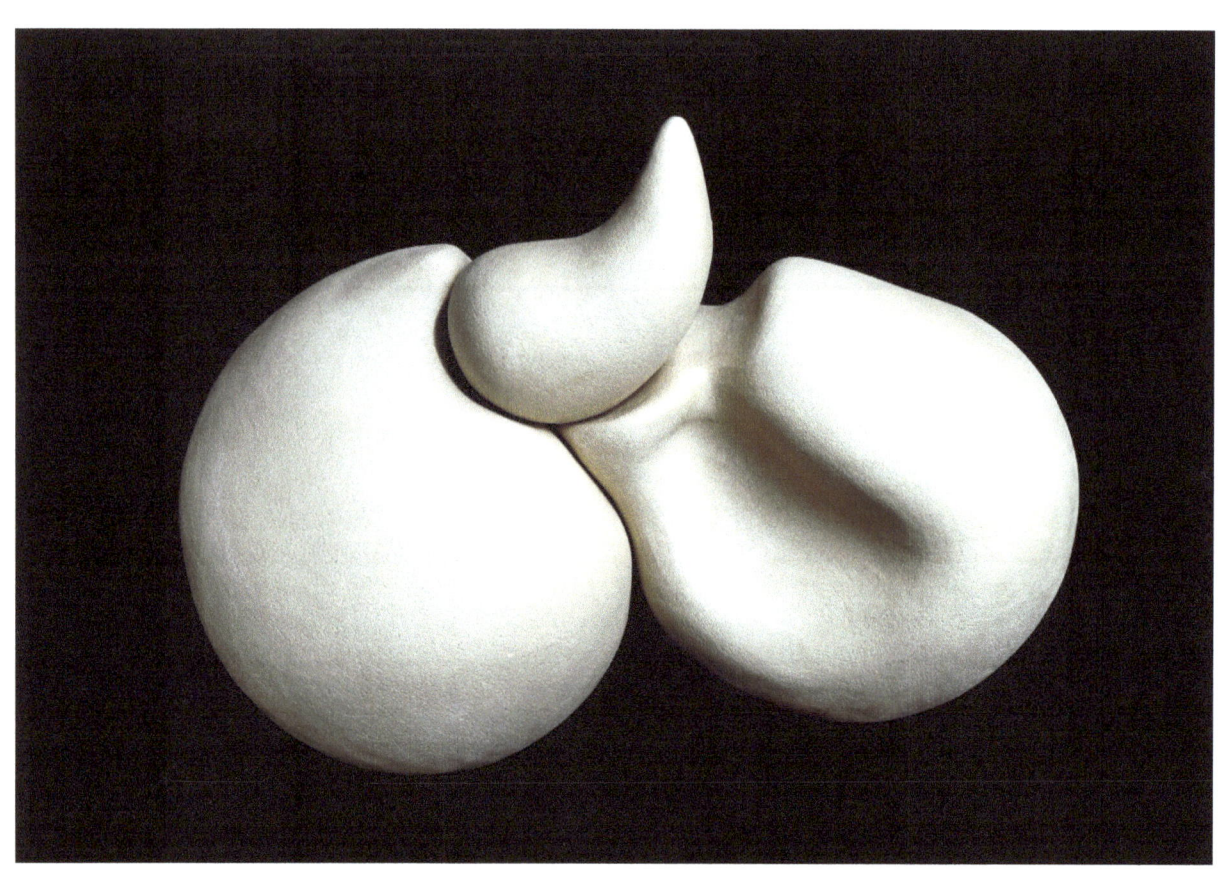

Jane Ogden-Swift

2015 BA (Hons) Three Dimensional Design, UCA Farnham

Jane's favorite tools are her hands and hand building with clay offers an intimate physical engagement with her material. The repetitive nature of making and shaping is almost meditative, the outside world recedes and she is focused on the form that is emerging from her working hands.

Like many artists Jane's experience of the natural world provides a rich source of visual inspiration. She is particularly interested in the collective and communal relationships with the world we live in; the influences and our responses, the spaces we create, the boundaries we establish and the marks we make on the landscape we live in.

Jane's current work stems from thinking about natural and manmade structures; their function, design and construction. The most compelling and thought-provoking were those that provided a living environment and this led to thoughts about how we live with each other as a family and within a community.

Jane's stoneware hand built and abstract sculptures explore her experience of human relationships. Closed curved forms offer protection whilst their shapes demonstrate the inevitable accommodations and metamorphosis that are part of the human dynamic.

Image: *Family II,* high fired stoneware clay finished with oil. Photographer: Anne Purkiss

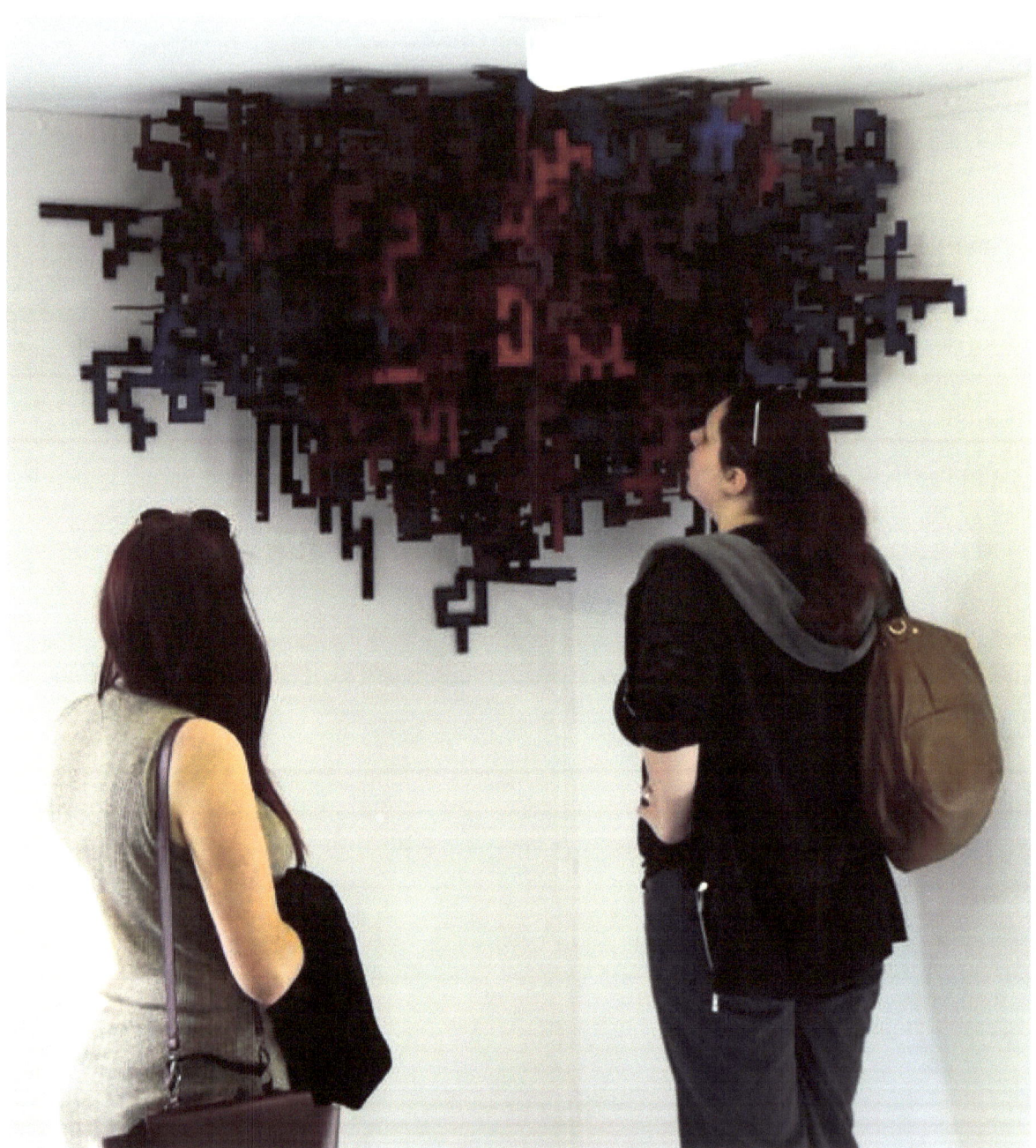

Henry Pucknell

2015 BA (Hons) Fine Art, UCA Farnham

"Today we reveal the reality that is behind visible things, thus expressing the belief that the visible world is merely an isolated case in relation to the universe."

(Paul Klee, 1920)

Henry is an artist based in Hertfordshire who works across mediums. His work deals with the mind, and how it processes oppressive feelings of anxiety and dread. He imagines that as with computer code, thoughts can be broken down into sterile strings of 0's and 1's and thus a narrow language of expression is utilised. Internal vulnerability is allowed to haunt the physical world, as a frantic, chaotic, yet ultimately functional mass or cloud.

Image: *Hollow Pipes Underwater,* laser cut MDF, matt car body paint. Photographer: Henry Pucknell

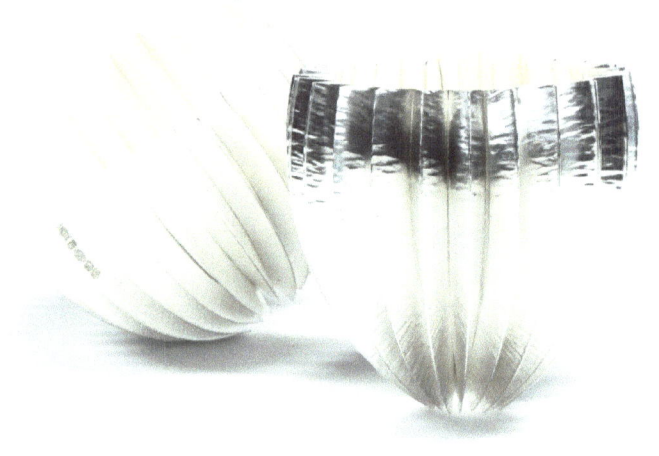

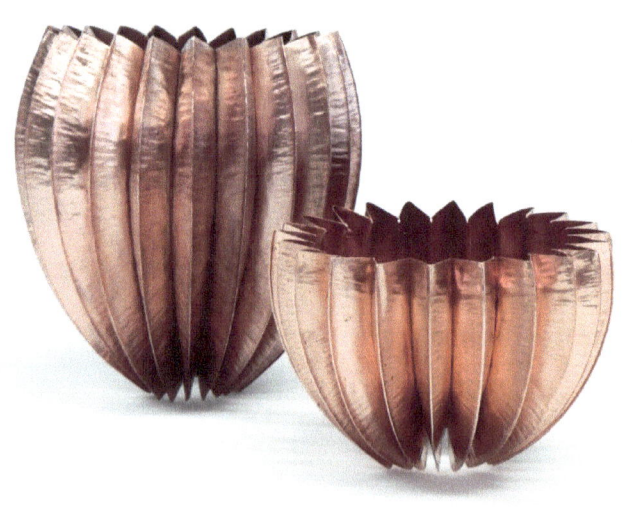

30

Emma-Jane Rule

2015 BA (Hons) Design Crafts, De Montfort University

Using the technique of foldforming alongside other traditional metalworking practices such as hammer forming and hand raising, Emma-Jane's work explores the malleable and intriguing natures of silver and copper.

Encouraging folded metal to curve and stretch in a designed direction, using hammers or a rolling mill, is a serendipitous way of working, which creates many opportunities for the metal to evolve and dictate the final form. Overcoming these challenges and learning how metal moves suits her playful and intuitive approach to metalworking.

The results are organic and tactile, interesting and precious three-dimensional forms, reflecting the undulating lines and rhythms found in the natural world, which is where Emma-Jane's inspiration is found. Additional surface textures, patinas and burnishing complement and enhance the metal's natural lustre and the hammered textures created during the making process.

Emma-Jane's work is aesthetic and sculptural, with a nod towards function. Select pieces of foldformed silver jewellery, echoing the techniques used, compliment the main collection. Her creations are unique and bespoke pieces, no two will ever be identical and her hope is to introduce her contemporary silver and metal work as pieces of luxury to brighten the everyday and treasured heirlooms for the future.

Emma is the winner of the Goldsmiths' Craft & Design Awards in 2016.

Image: *Prickles Pods,* copper and silver. Photographer: Dave Usher

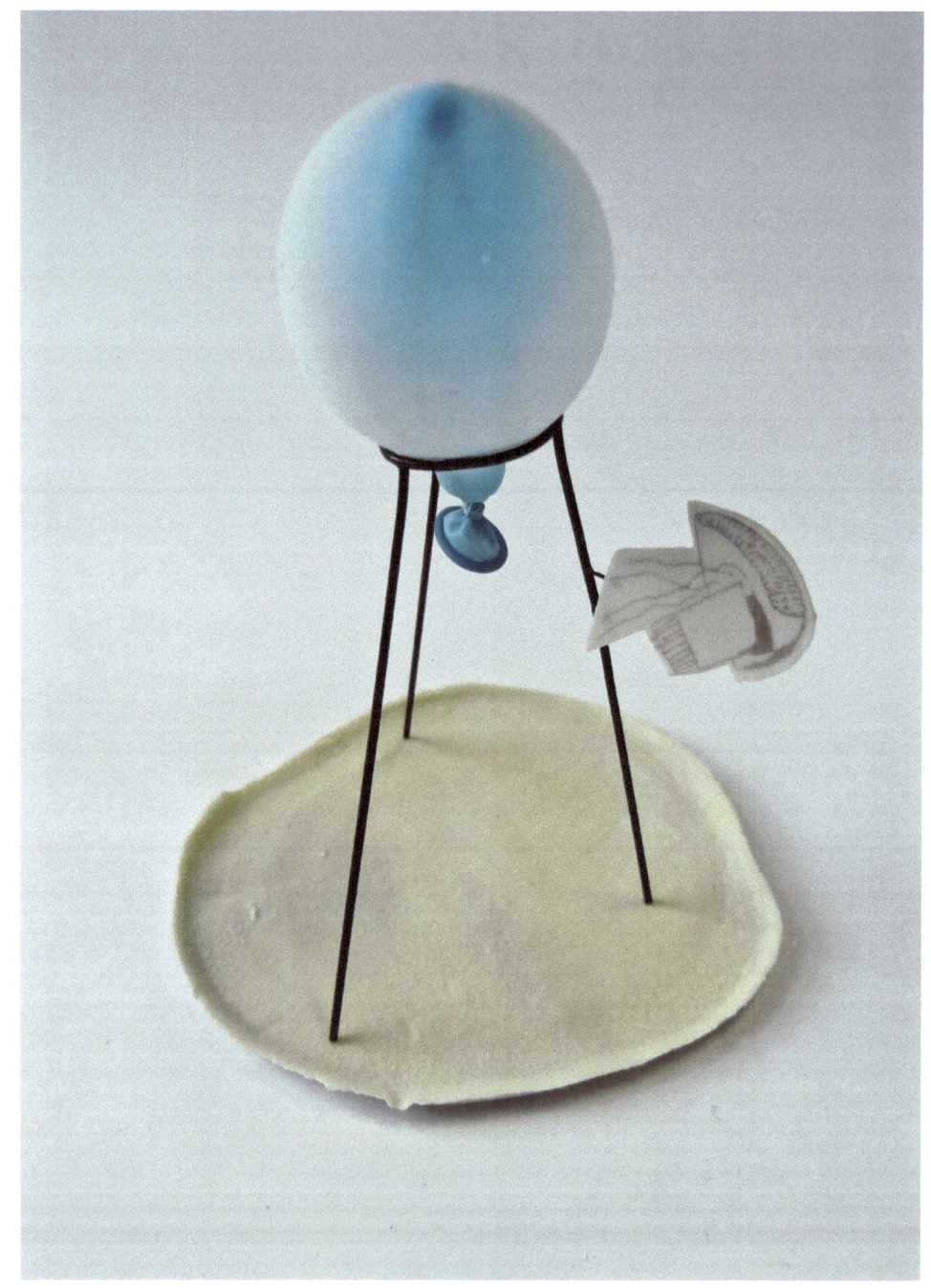

32

Emily Stapleton-Jefferis

2014 BA (Hons) Decorative Arts, Nottingham Trent University

Emily is interested in the pursuit of beauty. She aims to create objects and environments with a sense of narrative and play, actively engaging with viewers to stir memories, emotion and new perceptions of objects and places. Emily's work often responds to specific locations and the journeys within those spaces. The relationship that is then created between object and place really interests and excites her.

Emily's work is rooted in drawing, as a way of gaining inspiration, developing and refining objects and as an entity within itself. This interplay between 2D and 3D often creates interesting and surprising results, with the two actions being inextricably linked. Whilst drawing she loves to explore mark making as well as directly representing her surroundings, through combining these two styles and incorporating clay she can create layered and visually rich work.

The Japanese aesthetic of Wabi Sabi also underpins much of Emily's work, through the importance and appreciation for subtlety, spontaneity, imperfection, irregularity and inspiration from nature. Often the work she makes is rather small in scale, acting to draw the viewer in, as one must move closer to the work in order to discover its intricacies.

Image: *Undefined* series, porcelain and metal. Photographer: Emily Stapleton-Jefferis

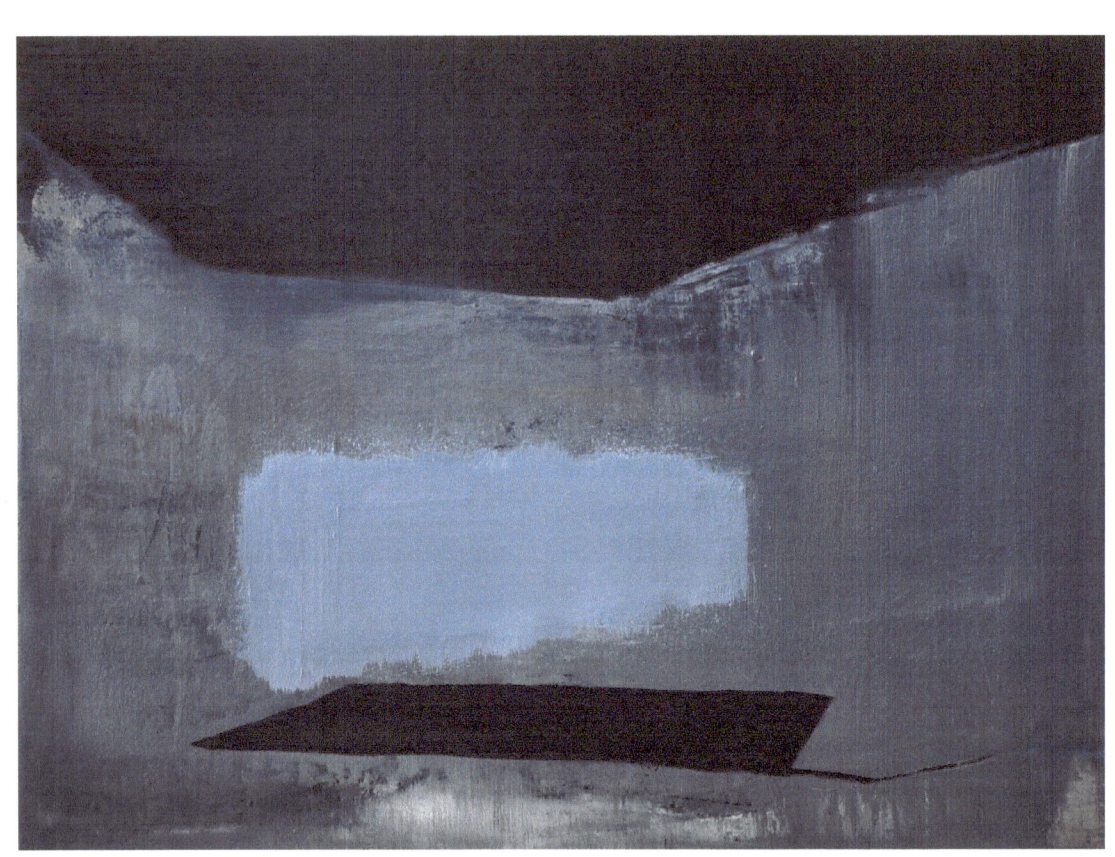

Mircea Teleaga

2016 MFA Painting, Slade School of Fine Art

2013 BA (Hons) Fine Art and Illustration, Coventry University

Mircea's works are a kind of introspective way of understanding recent history and its implications today. He looks at landscapes and ruins of his native post-communist Romania in order to start a painting. The ambiguity of historical events and the multiple points of view, from which a problem can be seen, has made his works more and more abstract and 'confusing'. A sense of schizophrenia is essential to Mircea's work. He has to deal with imagery that is part of his personal memories where also nostalgia is involved and imagery and historical information that records important, traumatic events of the 20th century having taken place.

He has found painting to perfectly suit his needs. Mircea is fascinated by the similarity between the process of painting and history/archaeology. His paintings are layered; they reveal some things, but hide more than they reveal. Hiding is probably the most important aspect here; and the fact that the viewer is conscious that something is hidden from him.

Image: *Untitled,* oil on canvas. Photographer: Mircea Teleaga

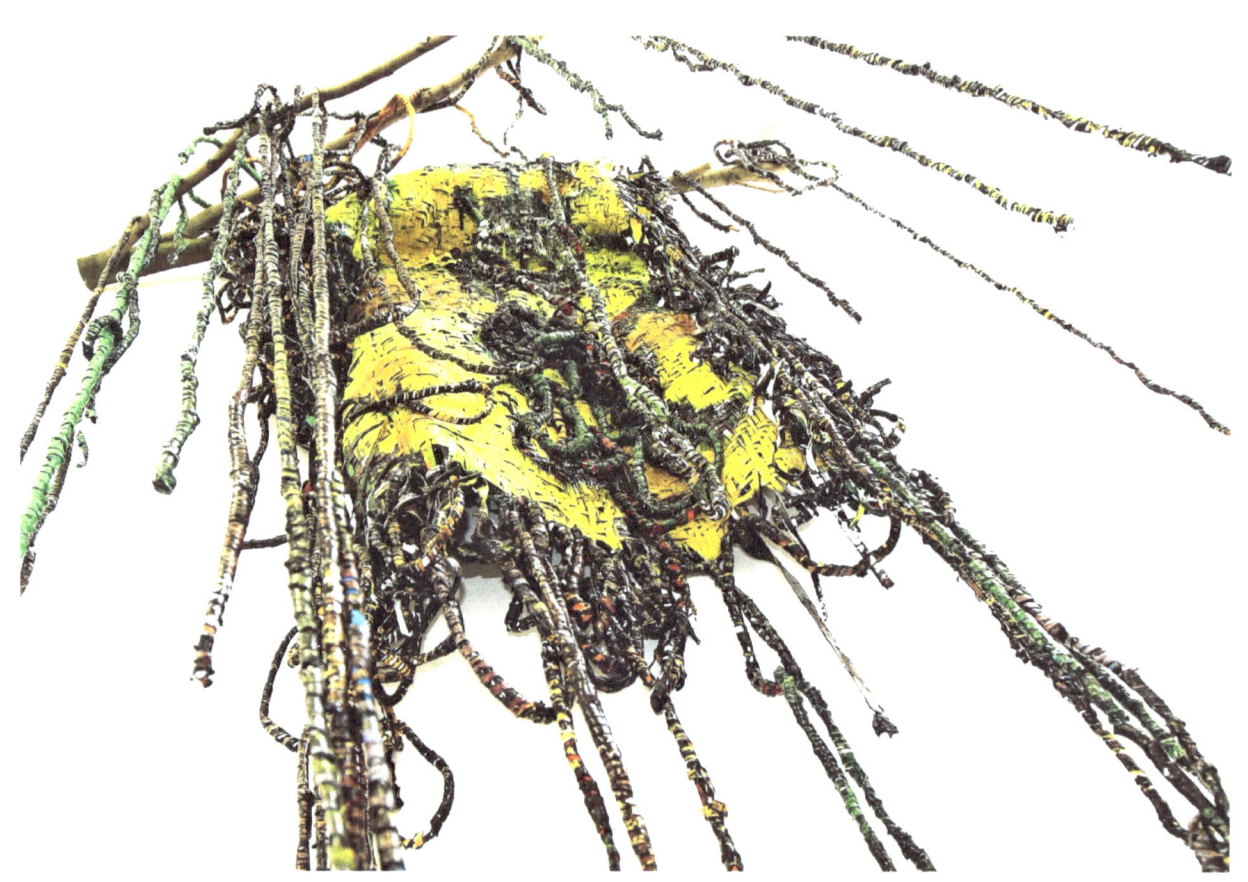

Albeiro Rojas Tomedes

2015 BA (Hons) Painting, Camberwell College of Arts (UAL)

Albeiro feels deeply for the natural and cultural riches of the Amazon where he grew up, as these are increasingly threatened by encroaching development. The colours, language, skills and heritage of the Amazon are a source of inspiration but the destructive forces of gentrification and globalisation that undermine nature's magnificent legacy are a driving force behind his work. Albeiro's has employed his distinctive technique with skins of gloss paint dried over a large area and then peeled to provide an unusual raw material for his work. The paint takes its own form and is liberated from the canvas. Freed from traditional constraints and artificial boundaries, the paint has been cut, ripped, peeled, folded, layered, twisted, rolled and woven, giving the paint independence and allowing a new form of expression.

The work is influenced by the impact of development on the natural environment and local culture. The de-construction of Albeiro's paintings echoes the destructive forces impacting upon the Amazon. Reflecting the slow erosion of native cultures, the paint is seen unravelling, scarred, torn and oozing out between layers. The shine of the black gloss paint symbolises the violence, pollution, anger and assault subjected upon beauty and nature. Albeiro's works occupy that 'in-between' space between painting and sculpture, stimulating thought about the role that paint can take and the form Albeiro has produced. These 'liminal' zones between painting and sculpture; dependency and independency; and the creative and destructive forces of mankind and nature are recurring aspects of Albeiro's work.

Image: *Liminal Incursion,* oil and gloss paint skins hung on a tree branch. Photographer: Albeiro Rojas Tomedes

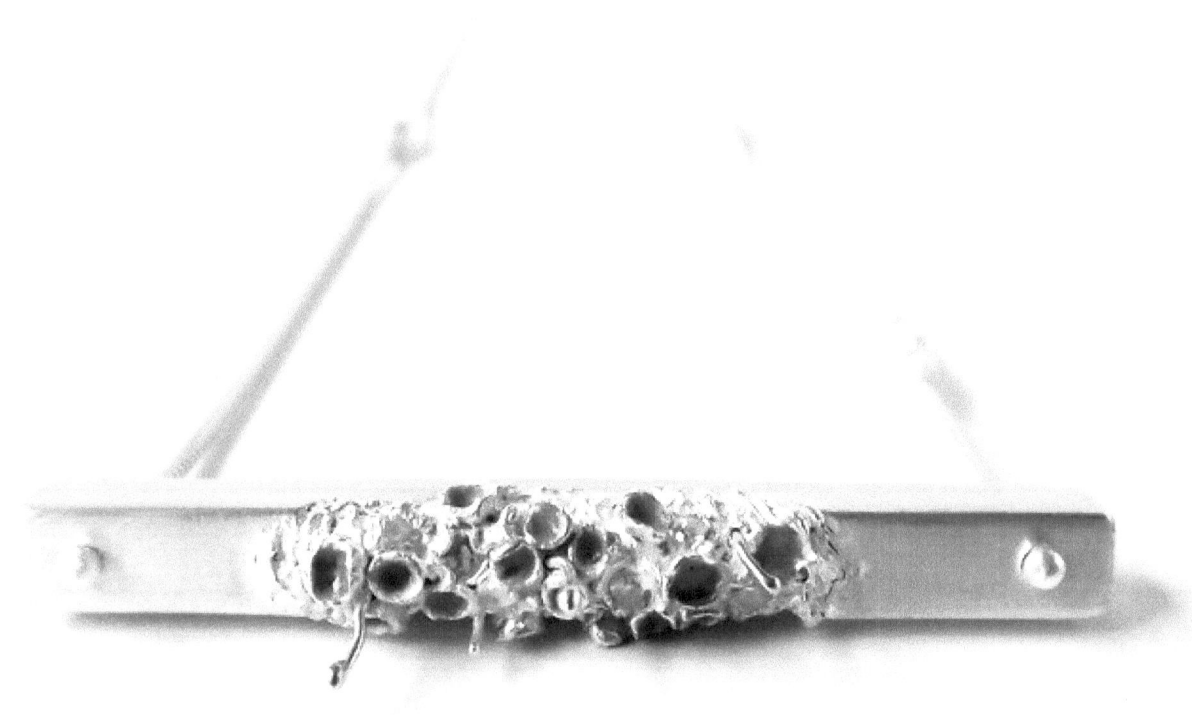

Melissa Yarlett

2015 BA (Hons) Contemporary Craft, University of Central Lancashire

Based in the North West Melissa gathers natural growths and formations from the local woodlands and mountains whilst exploring and climbing. She is greatly inspired by the mystery of Scandinavian folklore and natural growths such as Lichen, Moss and Rock formations - the most beautiful details are often the ones we overlook every day.

With a love for delicate and tiny details Melissa handcrafts bespoke pieces of jewellery using recycled silver that is then combined with Enamel, hidden stones and natural materials. Melissa makes each piece individually and her work is never cast or reproduced so no two pieces are the same, each with its own identity.

The 'Spore' collection features clean shapes and Lichen-like growths that have been crafted out of silver, which contrast and enhance one another. The aim of the collection is to capture nature taking back the material, instead of decaying the material is growing and transforming, being given new life and purpose.

Image: *Lichen Explosion Necklace*, silver and 24k gold. Photography: Melissa Yarlett

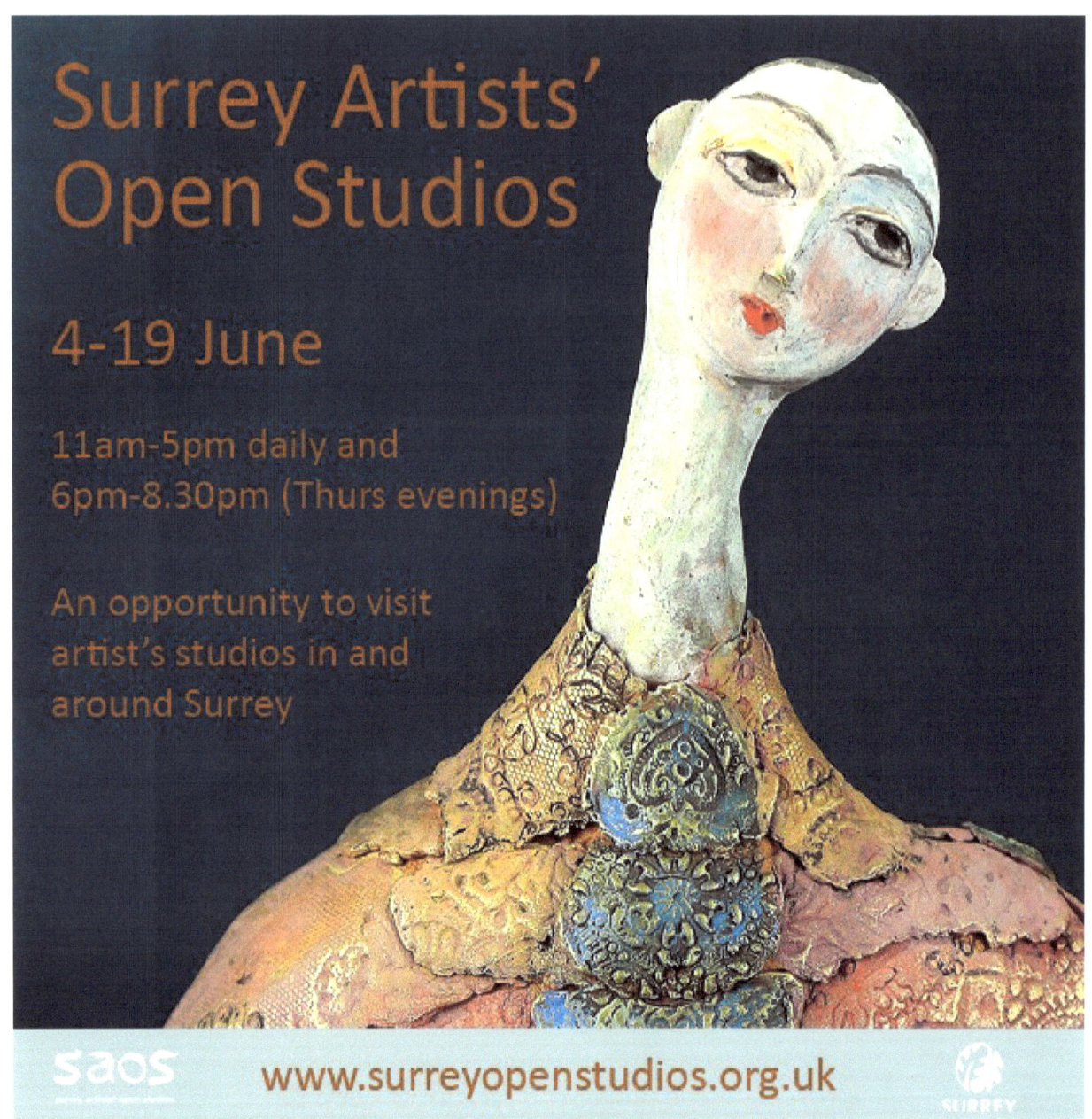

www.ingramcontent.com/pod-product-compliance
Lightning Source LLC
Chambersburg PA
CBHW051106180526
45172CB00002B/798